Preparing
the Thoroughbred

Preparing the Thoroughbred:

A TRAINER'S GUIDE

Anthony S. Coma

SOUTH BRUNSWICK AND NEW YORK:
A. S. BARNES AND COMPANY
LONDON: THOMAS YOSELOFF LTD

© 1972 by A. S. Barnes and Co., Inc.

A. S. Barnes and Co., Inc.
Cranbury, New Jersey 08512

Thomas Yoseloff Ltd
108 New Bond Street
London W1Y OQX, England

Library of Congress Cataloging in Publication Data

Coma, Anthony S
    Preparing the thoroughbred.

    1. Racehorse training. 2. Thoroughbred horse.
I. Title.
SF351.C64   636.1'08'88   75-37808
ISBN 0-498-01075-9

Printed in the United States of America

Contents

Preface

When I met her, she wasn't much of a "looker." In fact, she was rather dirty. She certainly wasn't proud and didn't seem to care much about life itself. But we both had a common interest . . . horse racing. She had never been a winner . . . in fact, she was a confirmed loser.

We spent much time together at the track. Yes, we spent a vacation together. Morning, noon, and night . . . breakfast and dinner were spent with each other. We learned much about winning and losing. We were lucky and won three races that year. We also had three second place finishes.

It was great and we had fun. Both of us felt good at finally being successful at a very hard game . . . the races. We decided to try again.

We thought we had a winner when all of a sudden a pain shot through her back leg. The move she made to win the race was voided when a foot from another horse completely severed her tendon. Still she ran. She finished . . . outdistanced.

The vet said she was through . . . she would never walk again. The message was clear . . . she had to be put down. The vet administered the lethal dose . . . and still she proudly stood. Countless time elapsed before she fell. Still she tried to win the game of life. Another dose was given . . . and there she lay . . . vanquished by the hypocrisy of "racing luck." Just a few races and her career was over. The winner . . . and yet, the loser.

It was over. We had so soon come to a parting of company. But she had changed. She had become a winner. Yes, it was a great romance. We both had given our best. We had been loyal and true to each other. She had given all she could . . . including her life.

And so this too shall pass. Billies Hostess is gone. Just another horse . . . I think not. Sometimes it takes "just a horse" to show what "effort" and "heart" really mean.

We had only 11 dates at the track. They were important. But being with her was most important. She wanted to live life to the fullest and was proud to be a winner. And it all ended where it had started . . . in the dirt.

The above eulogy reflects the feeling the author had for one of his thoroughbreds. It should also explain why the author wanted to write this work.

Preparing the Thoroughbred provides horse owners and trainers with some of the important basics: naming a thoroughbred, the importance of weight in the racing industry, feeding a horse, gelding a horse, loading a horse on a van, bringing a horse up to a race, reading form and correctly placing your horse, the use of drugs in training, horse ailments and treatments, and racing luck.

As will be restated later, constant attention must be given to the horses in your care. Effort and hard work are essential ingredients in this care. When there is any doubt in your mind, a veterinarian should be consulted. A horse can only give you that of which he is capable.

Remember, there is no guarantee your horse will ever be a winner. But, a horse, proper racing conditions, correct weight, and most of all, racing luck may give you the thrill of being in the winner's circle.

Introduction

It is hoped that the reader has read the eulogy included in the preface of this work and that he will understand the great part emotion plays in the ownership and care of a thoroughbred horse.

There are no promises or guarantees contained in this work. The facts, opinions, knowledge, and, most important, the experiences gained in the racing industry are as meaningful as anyone could want.

It is hopeful that many readers will, in some manner, either inherit, barter, trade, or "cuff" a thoroughbred. Once the decision of being a part of a thoroughbred horse has been made, it can only mean that the desire to stand in the winner's circle will become a complete penchant in that person's life. To stand in the winner's circle can only be accomplished if the thoroughbred has "four fleet feet." The complete, single idea that caused this work to be written is exactly that; some basic knowledge and opinion is being expressed by the author in order that the reader can evaluate in his own mind what he wishes to do to cause his thoroughbred to have "four fleet feet."

The thoroughbred racing industry, for lack of a better description, has been an enigma since the beginning of time. From the famous chariot races to present-day racing, the importance of competition has created in the hearts of owners the fond dream of having the best horse at a certain place and at a certain time.

9

The author was fortunate enough to spend a few neophyte years experiencing the many aspects of thoroughbred ownership, among them training, grooming, and caring for a thoroughbred. From mucking the stall, to standing in the winner's circle, to being the Chairman of the Board of Directors of the New Jersey School of Horsemanship . . . all came about through experiences and extreme feeling for one particular thoroughbred horse.

The many-faceted aspect of the importance of weight in the industry will be briefly discussed in order that the reader will be able to understand the importance of weight at various levels . . . be it the weight of the horse itself, the weight of the jockey or the weight necessitated by the conditions of the race.

The seemingly simple task of loading and unloading a horse onto a van may create many more problems than the average reader may think. This important area of the racing industry will be discussed.

Gelding a horse, an area fraught with apprehension many times in the racing industry, will be discussed with an attempt to explain the various thoughts of the author related to this matter. There are many ramifications of the problems that would bring the reader to decide upon this major decision. Some of these will be, hopefully, included in this area.

As there is no dictated way to feed a thoroughbred, the most accepted procedures of thoroughbred feeding will be discussed in another area of this work. Again, there are so many factors that enter into this area, that the most widely-accepted feeding procedures at certain situations in the life and time of the thoroughbred will be discussed.

When the reader has experienced the above areas of concern necessary in order to arrive at the threshold of racing, he will then be interested in understanding current thoughts

relating to procedures of preparing a horse for a race. Of
course, age, size, development and other factors bring
about various degrees of training. Some training programs
will be brought to the reader for his discernment and,
hopefully, his acceptance. While the author has deep feelings concerning the use of weight in the training program
of four year olds and older, he does conform to the generally-
accepted training programs, particularly in young horses.
Based on experience with his favorite four year old, the
author found a rather unique program involving the use of
a rider whose weight far exceeded that of normally-accepted
standards. Having been involved with human athletes in
various sports, the method of over-burdening athletes with
weight had proven so successful that the idea of a rider
whose weight was far in excess of normally-accepted standards proved, at least in the instance of one thoroughbred,
to be successful. However, the various programs for preparing a horse for a race will not deal with this weight
concept. There is no doubt in the author's mind relating to
the weight programs therein described relating to younger
horses. It is hoped that the reader will, on the basis of his
own experiences, choose the · program best suited for his
thoroughbred.

When a horse is finally ready for a race, it is important
that he is placed in the best possible situation in order for
him to win. Learning to read the form of the other horses
on the grounds may enable you to plan strategy and gain
knowledge needed to win. Chapter seven will deal with
this topic.

The use of drugs in training is an area in which the
author feels much reluctance on which to comment. The
urgency of getting the horse to the races necessitates many
practices which violate common sense. The expediency of
racing two year olds proves that money is more important

than the physical and natural development of a thoroughbred. The three year old races, namely the Kentucky Derby, the Preakness and the Belmont again reaffirm the fact that the natural maturation of a horse is not the most important factor in the racing industry . . . winning a very large purse is. If, in fact, the age of four was the magical age at which the big three races were offered, and perhaps the age of three was the first racing age for thoroughbreds, then the large number of injuries incurred by thoroughbreds would not leave such a nasty feeling in the minds of persons genuinely caring about the health and welfare of the horses. And so this area dealing with the use of drugs will be offered with tongue-in-cheek and will be brief, for the author hopes that the reader will understand the nature of the author's feelings regarding this area.

The last area in this work reflects the most serious efforts engaged in by the author. The chapter dealing with horse ailments and treatments reflects countless hours involved in every possible area of experiences related to horse ailments. While some areas may reflect concern on the part of the reader, it should be realized that every opinion expressed is that of the author and is based on his experience, not only with his own horses, but with the experiences of others caring for thoroughbreds. The information is based on years of experience in the field. Just as with humans, very few "specialists" can agree on the treatment of an injury; so, the age-old action of trial-and-error also applies to the care of a thoroughbred.

Preparing the Thoroughbred is offered to the reader with the sincere and deep hope that if just one concept or idea will be meaningful in the care of the reader's thoroughbred, the work will far exceed the fondest hopes of the author.

Preparing
the Thoroughbred

1
Naming a Thoroughbred

There are many aspects to be considered in the naming of
a thoroughbred. The process is not as simple as many
believe. All names are subject to the consideration and
approval of the stewards of the Jockey Club and are usually
limited to 16 letters and not more than three words. All
spaces and punctuation marks count as though they were
letters. It is illegal to use a name that has been used in the
previous 15-year period, either to stud or in racing. Further
restrictions are: the use of names whose spelling and pro-
nunciation are similar to those already in use, names of
illustrious or notorious persons, trade names, or names hint-
ing advertising. In order to name a horse after a living
person, the written consent of that person must be filed with
the Jockey Club.

Usually, owners will submit three names in the event
that the Jockey Club might disapprove of the first choice.
Often all three names may be turned down and three more
must be submitted. In years gone by, the names reflected
the breeding. This practice is still followed but not as often
as in the past.

To change the name of a thoroughbred, once again, three
names must be submitted to the Jockey Club and a longer
period of time is needed (usually about six months) for the

change to come through. When the horse finally resumes racing, the new name and "formerly run as —————" will appear on all racing documents.

When the horse's name is submitted to the Jockey Club, the Registrar's Office requires that the color and other markings be described. Colors are officially described as follows:

BAY: Varies from a light yellowish-tan (light bay) to a dark rich shade, almost brown, and, between these, a bright mahogany color (blood bay). Bays always have a black mane and tail as well as black points.

BLACK: If any doubt arises in distinguishing between dark brown and black, the black can be determined by noting the fine black hair on the muzzle.

BROWN: Sometimes difficult to distinguish from black or dark bay, but can be distinguished by noting the fine tan or brown hairs on the muzzle or flanks.

CHESTNUT: Varies from a dark liver color to a light washy yellow, with the brilliant red-gold and copper shades in between. A chestnut never has a black mane, tail or points.

GRAY: Mixture of white and black hairs; sometimes scarcely distinguishable from black at birth, but becomes lighter with age.

ROAN: There are two classes: the red (or strawberry) class, which is produced by the intermingling of red, white and yellow hairs, and the blue class, produced by the intermingling of black, white and yellow hairs.

The predominate color among thoroughbreds is bay, with about 46% being of that color. Chestnuts run about 30%, browns 18%, blacks 3%, grays 2%, and roans 1%.

Markings are officially described as:

BLAZE: A larger white patch. If the patch spreads over the entire face, the horse could be described as having a "white face."

SNIP: Small patch on the lip or nose. This may be either white or flesh-colored. One also omits the term "white" in describing the markings of a coronet or fetlock, unless one speaks of "white socks" or "stockings," the meaning of which is obvious. There are other white body markings. Some of these are hereditary and others are the result of an injury over which the hair has grown white.

STAR: Small patch of white hair on the forehead. It is never called a "white" star, the adjective being assumed.

STRIP: White running part-way down the face.

STRIPE: Thin narrow mark running down the face to the bridge of the nose or below.

2
The Importance of Weight in the Racing Industry

There is much that can be said relative to the importance of weight in the racing industry. The most commonly-accepted theory in racing is that "weight brings them all together." The track handicapper, who assigns the weight in many instances, imposes poundage in order to make the race more "even." This weight assignment is studied carefully by trainers and others engaged in the "sport of kings."

Weight is also extremely important in the life of a jockey. The length of his career as a race rider is relative to his ability to maintain a certain weight. Most trainers will discontinue the use of a specific jockey if his weight constantly exceeds the weight either assigned or brought about by the conditions of the race. Apprentice riders, due to their relative inexperience, are allowed weight reductions on the basis of the number of wins they have achieved for the period of their first year of riding. Thus, sometimes, in order to have his horse carry less weight, a trainer feels as though the inexperience of the rider will not negate the performance of his horse. In some instances, especially in young horses, some trainers feel as though there is less chance to have their horse injured with the "weight off." Sweat boxes are common at many tracks and show how important it is for a jockey to maintain his weight. The importance of weight may vary, for a horse's physical condition is either improving or on the downgrade. When a horse is "going well," he may shoulder the extra weight without too many problems. Conversely, when a horse is on the downgrade, the weight will hurt him more substantially. It has often been stated in thoroughbred racing that there is a point at which an extra pound of weight is the "straw that broke the camel's back."

The actual weight of the thoroughbred at various ages is also a very important part of racing. Horses are of all colors, sizes and shapes, but, at various stages of a horse's career, his weight is an important aspect to be considered if his performance is to be effective. A thoroughbred's weight usually reflects his conformation or, more commonly, his body build.

At birth, and as a foal, a thoroughbred's body is short and his legs are long. When humans are born, an announcement is usually sent reflecting the weight of the newborn. But in thoroughbred racing, the breeder is much more concerned with the conformation and general health of the thoroughbred, rather than his weight. At some breeding farms, very little attention is paid to weight. At others, weight bears consideration, an average weight of a yearling being about 860–900 pounds.

As a two year old, the body and the legs of the horse grow at the same rate. Surprisingly enough, the weight does not increase greatly. Usually the weight of a two year old will range between 900 and 1,000 pounds.

As a three year old, the legs and withers grow more rapidly so that at this age the height appears slightly in excess. Weight also increases at this age.

In thoroughbred racing, the distribution of weight is very important. Leverage can account for the stride of the thoroughbred. Some thoroughbreds, when at top speed, can maintain a stride from 25 to 28 feet.

The body of a horse can be separated into seven distinct parts. They are the trunk, four legs, the neck and the head. The distribution of weight in these seven areas is extremely important in the performance of a thoroughbred.

As a horse matures into a four year old, its body lengthens still further. When a thoroughbred is "unwound" and sent to a breeding farm for stud duty he will gain more weight as his training grind is over. Many stallions then grow to a weight of between 1,300 and 1,400 pounds.

3
Feeding a Thoroughbred

It has been reported that the annual feed bill for horses in the United States is in excess of $2 billion. More than $70 per horse is spent on yearly vitamin supplements and other health aids. There are many discrepancies and various theories regarding the feeding of a horse.

Nutrition is as important in the growth and development of thoroughbreds as it is in humans. However, certain physiological limitations, which will be stated later, cause problems in thoroughbreds. There is no magic formula or set rule on how much food is to be given to a thoroughbred. As will be stated many times in this work, each horse is an individual and must be treated accordingly. Thus, observation, knowledge of a horse's physiological limitations, and common sense are extremely important in the feeding of a thoroughbred.

Northern oats, yellow corn, wheat bran and barley, a little salt on the side, and the very best legume hay available are still the ultimate feed. The most important adjuncts to the feed box are grass and water. Well-fertilized grass, preferably bluegrass, is the answer to the mineral needs of a thoroughbred. Feed is very important in the development of thoroughbreds because they will start training at the tender age of about 18 months and will be in serious training when they are two years old. Thus, the nutritional aspects of feeding must begin as they are foaled and continue throughout the life of a thoroughbred. Their size and development will reflect the way they are fed and will aid greatly in more functional performances. In human beings, we have heard of the "basic seven" needed for proper diet. In thoroughbreds, it is many times not a question of "what" but rather "how much."

So in thoroughbreds there must also be a balance of food nutrients. Very little is known about the mineral requirements of a horse, but it is generally accepted that calcium, phosphorus, magnesium, sodium, chlorine and potassium are necessary additives in the thoroughbred's diet.

Vitamins are also essential additives. Vitamin A, or Carotine, is important to a thoroughbred. Lack of it can lead to night blindness, poor hoof growth, colic or reproductive failures. Fresh pasture and a natural diet usually provide adequate amounts of Vitamin A. But when hay is cut, it begins to lose its Vitamin A so much that fifty percent is lost over a single winter. The hay fed from January 1 on probably contains no more than half of its original Vitamin A. Horses also need the fat-soluble Vitamins D, E, and K as well as the water-soluble B-complex group.

Certain basic and recognized procedures in feeding a thoroughbred are commonly practiced. A horse should be watered before being fed due to the fact that watering afterward impairs the thoroughbred's digestion and is liable to cause colic. It is virtually impossible to give a thoroughbred too much water and thoroughbreds usually consume four to ten gallons daily. Unfortunately, the stomach of a horse is relatively small compared to other animals and to his own size. This necessitates frequent feedings and will usually require the person caring for a horse to feed him four times per day. Thus, by multiple feedings and in small quantities, a person will be able to prevent the horse from becoming ravenous and gulping his food down, which would thus cause him to get indigestion.

Just as a trainer must try to find out how much work his horse can endure, so must he determine the amount of food each horse in his care should have. Hay is the most recognized food for a thoroughbred and a horse can subsist on it alone.

The most common grain fed to horses is oats. The necessary elements for building muscle and adding flesh are contained in oats, which are said to be appetizing to the thoroughbred. In light training periods, horses may eat ten quarts of oats, while in hard training, they may eat 11 to 14 quarts. Again, this varies with the individual thoroughbred. It is suggested that bright white oats with a polished shine be selected. Watch for dark or stained seeds. These oats are weathered. Also look closely for brownish-colored oats. This condition is called "bin burn." It results from oats being improperly stored due to excessive moisture and heat. Both "weathered" and "burned" oats are bitter and horses reject them. The best way to detect damaged oats is to squeeze the groat from the hull and check to see if the damage to the outer husk penetrated the groat. Healthy, rich oats have a sweet taste. To check, remove the groat and chew it. After trying this a few minutes, the reader will be able to taste the difference. Another clue is odor. Many times oats are stored for long periods under improper conditions. These oats develop a musty or stale odor. It would be unwise to purchase or use oats with an unusual odor. At race tracks, older oats are thoroughly cleaned, recleaned and magnetized to remove all foreign material, other grains, chaff and dust.

Most trainers feed their horses similarly. The diet consists mainly of varieties of hay, such as heavy clover, light clover and timothy mixture, and light straight timothy. Oats can be either light or heavy, crushed or whole. The light, crushed oats are more easily digested.

When a trainer uses mash it usually consists of a mixture of bran, corn, chopped carrots and oats with the addition of blackstrap molasses and lime water. When the weather becomes hot, corn is generally eliminated from the mash. Grass, when available, is essential, as well as fresh water, chilled but never too cold. Alfalfa hay is occasionally included in the diet of a thoroughbred. After a hard race or a stiff workout, mashes usually are the order of the day. At other times, dry feed may be used.

With the rise of costs involved in the thoroughbred industry, it is natural for horsemen to seek ways of reducing expenses. Many times, unfortunately, the feed bill is a victim in an economy move. This makes little sense, as top quality oats are richer and your horses will require less per feeding. Your bills will average out about the same.

It cannot be emphasized too often that overfeeding is a serious mistake. A thoroughbred's appetite should be tempted by the presentation of a variety of well-prepared food. No thoroughbred should be forced to eat or drink. The trainer will be easily able to ascertain how hungry his horse is and whether or not his thoroughbred requires food at certain times.

In conclusion, a horse needs varied things in his overall diet. He needs the fat-soluble Vitamins A, D, E, and K and the water-soluble Vitamin B-complex group. Water is extremely important. Six important minerals are needed: calcium, phosphorus, sodium, chlorine, and potassium, in addition to the minerals magnesium and selenium. A thoroughbred's normal diet, whether pasture, hay, grain or a commercial feed, may not be enough and may short-change him. Some combination of these nutrients and vitamin-mineral supplements added to his diet are nutritional necessities which protect a horse from the oversights of owners or the inconsistencies of Mother Nature. Like a human, a horse is what he eats. How well he will run is greatly influenced by his diet.

4
Gelding a Horse

Throughout the history of thoroughbred racing, there have been reports of racing success achieved through gelding. Perhaps the most famous of gelded horses was the one and only Kelso. Kelso, Mrs. DuPont's wonderful thoroughbred, was unable to win a race until the age of five . . . and then only after Kelso was gelded.

There are many reasons a horse will be gelded. If a young colt cannot keep his mind on training, he will be so inconsistent in his performances that the trainer cannot tell from one day to another how he will perform. When a horse is of this nature, the risk of gelding him becomes a necessary one in order that his performances will show consistency. The possibility of negating the horse's ability is present. But, more often than not, gelding, in this situation, proves fairly successful.

Many young colts have a masturbation problem. Again, as was stated above, the horse in this condition will masturbate to the point where his effectiveness leaves much to be desired. Many trainers consider gelding when this situation occurs. Another cause for gelding is that a horse is overly unruly and at times mean. Some young colts, due to reasons of their own, are so high strung and cantankerous that they will make every effort to be "kings" of their stalls and will challenge anyone entering with threat of bodily violence. Some young colts have been known to actually hurt persons entering their stall for any reason. When a 1,000 to 1,200 pound young male horse decides he is going to pin an intruder onto the wall, he will do so. When he wants to kick someone, very few will be able to stop him. Much attention must be made by the person caring for a horse to avoid getting behind a horse, thus partially eliminating some of this danger. When a horse is overly mean and cantankerous, there is little that can be done to prepare him for the races. Gelding in this situation is almost a necessity . . . the results have to be ascertained at a later date.

Other young colts have a problem of glandular and physical growth. For various reasons, gelding becomes a necessity in order to go on with the very serious program of training and getting your horse to the races. In this situation, it is sometimes physically expedient to geld a horse. It is a gamble, but it is probably your only choice.

There are other reasons why a horse may be gelded, but the reader may be able to ascertain some rationale for the entire concept. Horses may be gelded at any age, as was Kelso. However, most horses are gelded as yearlings. Some reasons for this might be that most owner-breeders realize the "class" of their horse and know that the business of training will go easier if their horse is gelded. Owners of "class" colts rarely will geld their horses until a behavioral pattern is ascertained and then only out of necessity.

Obviously, colts that exhibit any of the above or exhibit bad habits will probably be gelded if their "bad habits" would deem them unfit for training and for eventual thoroughbred racing.

There is no great crime, in the opinion of the author, in

gelding a horse if the reason is one of desiring a more functional racing thoroughbred. The author would not geld a "class" horse until he was sure that the horse would not conform to measured standards of thoroughbred training. Once a strain of non-conformity was established, gelding would become a necessity. It is the opinion expressed here, that any horse without potential either in breeding or as a stake horse should be gelded. There are reasons that support this statement. You will get much more useful service over a longer period of time out of a horse that has been gelded. Colts, usually after the age of six, become extremely fractious and run very inconsistently. They run some good races and, unfortunately, some very bad ones. Generally, they run as they please. They are very inconsistent in their performances. They will bear in, bear out, sulk, lug in or generally behave as a totally unpredictable colt.

Geldings, to the contrary, can perform functionally at the age of nine and ten and will run consistently at that age. They have no sex problem and are easier to train and are much more consistent.

Sadly, the only chance for some horses ever to be useful performers is through gelding . . . but there is only a 50/50 chance.

In the process of gelding the risk exists that some of the competitiveness innate in the colt may disappear . . . to put it simply, he may lose some of his "heart." But this is just another challenge that is to be met if one desires to compete in thoroughbred racing.

5
Loading a Horse on a Van

Patience is the key to success . . . and perhaps the only way to lead some horses onto vans. Most thoroughbred horses know what they want to do and will attempt to do just that. You may know what you want them to do, but force and your ideas may not be enough to work in most situations involving loading a horse onto a van. It is of utmost importance that you do not get your horse "worked up." Calmness is important in this situation, to both horse and man.

The more upset the horse is, the less likely will be your success in loading him onto the van. Given enough patience, a horse will eventually walk onto the van.

A horse should be quietly walked towards the van. When the van is approached, the horse should be permitted to walk on . . . even if only one foot at a time. Some horses may be coaxed by gently laying straws or a broom lightly on their rear. A horse should never be whipped or beaten. Force will not work. Even if you only get a step every couple of minutes, you will eventually get the horse onto the van. Most persons work against themselves because of their impatience.

Horses are creatures of habit. It is extremely important

that the first experiences a horse has concerning loading are pleasant. If this is the case, usually after a few successful loadings the job should become more routine and less difficult.

Loading, however, is not a one-man job. It is extremely important to have someone else available to close the rear gate of the van as soon as the horse is loaded. This cannot be done too quickly. Many instances of horses backing out of the van and causing injury or running away are well recorded. One cannot underestimate the speed at which a horse is capable of backing out of a van. Once the horse has achieved this end, he will be a little more difficult to load the next time. When a horse has experienced no problem in entering a van, the job will become only one of loading him quickly on and off the van but much respect must continually be given to an animal weighing over 1,000 pounds.

While the process of loading a horse is a difficult one, conversely, unloading a horse is easier, but presents a different set of problems. Imagine yourself walking downstairs backwards. Much attention must be made to be sure that the person unloading is in complete command of the horse.

When thoroughbred horses become habituated to the routine of loading and unloading, relatively few problems will occur. Again, it must be emphasized that patience will be rewarded.

Loading a horse onto a van.

6
Preparing a Horse for a Race

There are many theories regarding the various programs of conditioning needed to get a thoroughbred ready for a race. Some of these will be discussed later in the chapter.

However, a basic premise held by the author bears stating at this time. Horses are individuals . . . not machines or wild animals. They are domestic animals and have their own ego and personality. It is important that anyone tending a horse keep this well in mind. It is the responsibility of the trainer or person caring for the horse to find out what a horse wants and what he is capable of giving. A thoroughbred, like any other domestic animal, needs to belong to someone. He has to be developed physically and psychologically. One of the most important components in the thoroughbred's makeup that has to be developed and cultivated is the will to win. This is particularly true in cheaply-bred horses. Usually, when a thoroughbred is bred well, the innate desire to win will be present due to his "class." However, even "class horses" can lose their will to win for a while. Whether or not the horse wants to run and win is the challenge of the individual person caring for the horse. Horses must be made to feel aggressive and important.

If this is not done, you will not have much more than a mechanical horse whose performance will be spotty at best. A horse with speed alone is not a race horse. It takes much more than just speed.

In the racing industry, grooms spend more time with individual thoroughbreds than anyone else. Therefore, they have a great deal to do with the development of the horse's personality. The importance of the role of groom cannot be too highly emphasized. Successful horses reflect successful trainers who reflect the hard and earnest work of grooms who care about the horses in their care. Therefore, grooms must be made to remember that each horse has an individual ego and must be treated as such. To be successful in handling horses, one must know and understand them. A basic knowledge of the physical makeup is essential, but will not produce a winner. Some thoroughbreds are timid and have to be made to feel as though they are "someone" and, as a result of this, they will become more competitive. Other thoroughbreds are extremely friendly and want all kinds of playful attention. Still others want attention, but not too much fondling or petting. Thus, the groom, who will spend more time with a thoroughbred than any other person, will have to get to know the horses in his care and what they want and require in order to give maximum performance. In a large thoroughbred operation, the trainer cannot possibly get to know all the horses in his charge. Therefore, he should make very sure that his most capable grooms handle his "best horses." The trainer should check on his grooms and ascertain whether they have given the "extra mile" in the care of the horses assigned them. The generalization is that the best grooms rub and care for the best thoroughbreds. The racing industry, at this writing, is in tremendous need of grooms. There are several schools throughout the country attempting to recruit and graduate qualified individuals to fill this tremendous void. In schools such as these, the candidates, upon successful completion of the courses, find instant employment. A good groom is a very valuable individual and his importance to the racing industry cannot be overestimated.

In the matter of developing ego and personality, it is in extremely poor judgment to allow a horse in your charge to get outrun badly two or three consecutive times. If this is allowed, you may take out all or some of the "heart" from that horse. It is especially important that in workouts you make sure that your horse is not outrun. In this way, it is possible to build up his ego and competitiveness. If it is still evident that your horse is going to be outrun in the workout, your exercise boy should be instructed to take back, or hold back, on your horse so that there will still be some doubt in the horse's mind about what he can do. It is of utmost importance that your horse must think that he had a chance to win.

In a race, of course, you must try to win. It is here that the true value of horsemanship comes into play. You must know your horse and as much as you can about other horses on the grounds. Do not overmatch your horse. When a horse is winning and confident, he may move up in "class." The horse's winning psyche will carry him a little further, perhaps, than his breeding would indicate. Conversely, when a horse is going off form, he either must be given a rest or lowered in "class." Be "horseman enough" to know your thoroughbred's value and run him where he belongs. Thus, your horse will be competing in the company of other horses where he has a chance to be successful.

When claiming a horse, it is important that you attempt to know, or successfully guess, the physical and psychological makeup of someone else's horse. When you feel that this horse is in shape and can win, a claim is in order. This, of course, can be classified as an educated guess. Horses definitely reflect those individuals caring for them. Poor handlers, in the end, will have poor horses. Once a horse's ego has been beaten down, it is a very hard and long road to reestablish his confidence and will to win. At this stage of the horse's psychological breakdown, it may be wise to turn him out and let him on his own for a while.

In the matter of bringing two year olds up to a race, an eight-week training period is recommended. Again, the author wishes to emphasize that there are numerous philosophies dealing with this matter and the reader will have to ascertain which works best for him. However, here is a suggested program:

In order to prepare your thoroughbred for concentrated work, you must first begin a legging-up program. This is similar to humans beginning a training-conditioning program leading to their competing in a particular sports event. To begin the legging-up program, horses should be galloped one mile a day. The distance should be increased during an eight-week period until the horse is galloping two miles a day. The intervals of work are two days of galloping and one of "breezing." A gallop is exactly what it says it is and "breezing" is when the horse is allowed to run at almost maximum, untouched, free will. The term "breezing," in the racing industry, means that the horse runs on his own and is not whipped or hand-urged by the rider. However, when breezing, a reminder is made to make sure that there will always be some doubt in the horse's mind of how fast he can run. Thus a certain amount of restraint should be exercised when breezing.

When your horse returns either from a gallop, breezing, or any type of workout, certain physical items should be checked, such as: how the horse comes back, whether his head is up and he looks spunky or whether his head is down and he appears weary, his reaction to food, and whether he appears dull-looking are some factors to be considered. Once you feel that the legging-up period is over, usually lasting eight-weeks for two year olds, you will want to begin more concentrated work for your thoroughbred. The following schedule is recommended:

Initially breeze a slow quarter mile.

Then breeze a quarter mile a little faster.

Then breeze a slow ⅜ of a mile.

Then breeze a quick quarter mile.

Then breeze a slow couple of ½ miles.

Then breeze a fast ⅜ of a mile.

Then breeze a slow ⅝ of a mile.

Then breeze a sharp ½ mile.

It is recommended that the horse is not pressed past a fast ½ mile work. It is also thought that a horse should not be worked farther than he has to run (two year olds). Again, the intervals should be two days of galloping and one of breezing. One must keep in mind that training schedules have to be altered to suit the horse. You cannot make him keep a strict schedule. He can only give you what he is capable of doing.

The following schedule is recommended for horses that have, for one reason or another, been away from the track. Again, a full legging-up period of eight weeks is recommended. Long, slow gallops are the order of the day at the beginning until you feel the horse is ready for "breezing." This is a little different than the procedure followed for two year olds. Alternating galloping and breezing are not recommended here. The horse should be galloping an easy two miles by the end of this eight-week period. Your legging-up program should have begun at one mile and increased, as the horse allowed, during the legging-up period. At the end of this period, the following schedule is recommended:

Breeze a ⅜ mile.
Breeze a quick ¼ mile.
Breeze a quick ⅜ mile.
Breeze a slow ½ mile.

As the breezing is increased, the gallops should be shortened until the horse is working ⅝ mile and galloping one mile. Then walk every third day. The intervals should be: gallop, breeze, walk. After four or five workouts you may occasionally "let him go" near the end of a work. But, it is not recommended to let the horse go "all out." The author wishes to again recommend to the reader that some restraint be used with his thoroughbred so that something is always left in the horse . . . there must be doubt in his mind about how fast he can run. You should be more interested in the condition in which your horse returns from these workouts. Some items to look for would be: is he playful, is his head up, and is he hungry? These items are what you should observe.

Conditioning is an extremely important item in the preparation of a horse for racing. Fast workouts do not prove anything. It is recommended that you ask a little less of the horse than you know he can give.

As has been stated previously, schedules vary. Some horses are worked out the morning they race. Others are walked around the barn until the day they race. Of course, these horses are fit. The recent Kentucky Derby and Preakness winner Canonero II proved to one and all that training techniques vary not only in this country but throughout the world. Conditioning is the important factor, not the speed of a workout, in getting your horse to be a winner.

7
Reading the Condition Book and Racing Form

It has often been stated that class and consistency go together. When racing at, for example, a $5,000 level, it is possible that if the same group horses were run against each other the outcome could produce several different winners on different occasions. On the other hand, when racing in allowance company, two or three horses can consistently win over a similar number of competitors. Thus, pace is not deemed as important as class. Pace is important as the claiming pace descends its scale. Class horses run fast enough to win. They are not interested in the time that it would take to win a race, but just winning it. There have been many tales of how one horse would look at three or four other horses who made a run at him square in the eye and the other horses would quit. The factors of the conditions of the race and the weight carried are also important in determining a winner.

Also to be considered are the track conditions. Again, breeding plays an important part. Where the background indicates good off-track performances or good grass performances, there is a strong likelihood that these traits will

39

appear in the offspring. When a horse has strictly a sprinting background in his breeding, it is unlikely that he will be able to carry that speed over 1 mile or 1-$\frac{1}{16}$ mile. Conversely, when a horse is bred by parents exhibiting long-distance backgrounds, the probability of his being a good sprinter is less likely. Thus, the luxury of ideal breeding usually can be afforded only by those owners with good financial backgrounds.

Knowing the other horses on the grounds was previously stated to be an important factor in the placement of one's horse. Also, the trainer should be able to understand basics in handicapping the racing form. He should understand that there are numerous track conditions which may affect the race. The following are some basic symbols which are important and must be understood:

fst: fast
fr: frozen
gd: good
sl: slow
sly: sloppy
my: muddy
hy: heavy

Races run on the turf (grass), including steeplechase and hurdle races, are indicated as hd: hard.

fm: firm
gd: good
yl: yielding
sf: soft

The trainer should also be able to denote the mud classifications listed below:

✳ fair mud runner
x good mud runner
⊗ superior mud runner

And when scanning through the recent workouts of other horses, he should be able to understand the various degrees of the workout. They are as follows:

b: breezing
d: driving
e: easily
h: handily
bo: bore out
o: all out
ro: ran out
u: eased up
g: worked from stall gate

The letters "tr.t" following track abbreviations indicate a horse worked on a training track. The abbreviations "t.c." indicate a turf course. All workouts are on the main track unless otherwise designated.

Points of call are also important in the trainer's knowledge of handicapping. In races of less than one mile (with the exception of the shorter sprints), the past performance line gives, in addition to the post position and the start, the position at the three-sixteenths or quarter-mile, three-eighths or half-mile, the stretch and the finish, as well as the margin by which the horse was leading or by which he was trailing the leader at those points of call. In races of one mile or more, the post position is retained, but the quarter-mile call is substituted for the start call. This is followed by his positions and leading (or beaten-off) margin at the next points of call, half-mile, pre-stretch, stretch and finish. The pre-stretch call in most races is made one-quarter mile from the finish and the stretch call, about one-eighth mile from the finish. Points of call vary according to the distance and are shown in the chart of the race from which the past performance line is derived.

The abbreviations used in the classifications of different types of races are as follows:

Allowance:	Allowance race.
Clm 10000:	Claiming race. (Entered for $10,000)
Stk 50000:	Claiming stakes. (Entered for $50,000)
f-M 10000:	Fillies or fillies and mares, maidens claiming. (Entered for $10,000)
Handicap:	Handicap
Hcp 10000:	Handicap, claiming (Entered for $10,000)
Inv.H'cap:	Invitational handicap. (overnight)
Md Allow:	Maidens, allowances
Md 10000:	Maidens, claiming. (Entered for $10,000)
Md.Sp.Wt.:	Maidens, special weight
Match R:	Match race
Clm °10000:	Optional claiming race—NOT entered to be claimed.
Clm 10000°:	Optional claiming race—WAS entered to be claimed.
Hcp °10000:	Optional claiming handicap—NOT entered to be claimed.
Hcp 10000°:	Optional claiming handicap—WAS entered to be claimed.
Spec'l Wt.:	Special weight
Alw 10000s:	Starter allowance race.
Hcp 10000s:	Starter handicap.
Md 10000s:	Starter maiden race.
Spw 10000s:	Starter special weight race.

In stakes races, with the exception of claiming stakes, the name or abbreviation of name is shown in the class of race column. For example, the Kentucky Derby would be shown as "Ky. Derby" or Excelsior Handicap as "Excels'r H." The letter "H" after name indicates the race was a handicap stakes. The same procedure is used for the rich invitational races for which there are no nomination or starting fees. The letters "Inv" following the abbreviation indicate that the race was by invitation only.

Two other factors may be of some importance to the trainer in his attempting to place his horses correctly. They are the speed ratings and track variant. Speed ratings are a comparison of the horse's final time in the race with the track record established prior to the opening of the meeting. If a horse equals that track record, he is given a rating of 100. One point is deducted for each one-fifth second slower than the track record. Thus a horse timed two and two fifths slower than the record receives a rating of 88 (100 minus 12). If a horse breaks the track record his speed rating exceeds 100. For example, if he is timed one-fifth second faster than the track record he receives a rating of 101. In computing beaten-off distance for speed ratings, fractions of one-half length or more are considered as one full length (one point). No speed ratings are given for steeplechase or hurdle events, for races of less than three furlongs, or for races where the earned speed rating is less than 25.

The track variant takes into consideration all of the races run on a particular day and could reflect either the quality of the competition, how many points below par the track happened to be, or both. The speed rating of each winner is added together, then an average is taken based on the number of races run. When there is a change in the track condition during the course of a program, the following procedure is employed in compiling the variant: races run on dirt tracks classified as fast, frozen, or good, and those listed as hard, firm or good on the turf, are used in striking one average. Strips classified as slow, sloppy, muddy or heavy on the dirt, or yielding and soft on the turf, are grouped for another average. If all the races on a program

are run in either one or the other of these general classifications, only one average is used. The lower the variant, the
faster the track or the better the quality of competition.

NOTE: A separate track variant is computed for races run
on the turf (grass), straight course races, and for races run
around turns at a distance of less than five furlongs. Races
run over the Tartan Track also receive a separate variant.

Basically speaking, after learning to read the form the
next step is thoroughly understanding the condition book.
If you have a maiden, place him in a maiden race. An
exception might be if your horse is very fit or there is no
maiden race available. However, if you put a maiden in an
allowance race, he will probably be beaten. He will be
competing against horses who have run one or more races.
Even if your maiden wins, he will be penalized later because
other races may offer allowance for non-winners other than
a maiden race. Thus, your horse will be ineligible for this
weight concession.

The next course to pursue after your horse wins its
maiden race is a race for non-winners of two races. After
his second win there will be plenty of races for horses that
have not won two races other than maiden or claiming.

There are plenty of filly races. As a two year old, an
especially sharp filly can tackle colts and do well. They
have a knack of leaving the gate quicker. But, as three
years olds, fewer fillies tackle colts. In races requiring
strength and stamina, the colts usually beat the fillies.

It is suggested that a trainer keep his fillies in mare and
filly races. Only now and then can an exceptional mare
face colts and beat them. If there are no filly-mare races,
you have no choice.

Claiming horses, as previously stated, must be carefully
placed. Horses worth $3,000 should be kept and run in their

class. A $7,000 horse should run for $7,000. It is true that there are times that a horse may win a notch or two above his actual level. However, the trainer should really know where the horse belongs and race him at that level. It is at this level that he will be most successful.

It is well to remember that losing a race is very important. Your horse, if constantly beaten by better horses, will become discouraged and may not be able to win any kind of race . . . at his level or below. Conversely, if you find easy spots for your horse whereby he wins several races, he may "move up" and be successful.

As a trainer, you are charged with the responsibility of keeping complete records. You should determine quickly what horse you have and which earnings make him eligible for certain races. Maiden races pose no problem, but eligibility conditions of other races become more complicated.

Weights pose another problem. Certain horses race better with light weight. The trainer is faced with the problem of selecting races where the conditions will be such that his horse will carry light weight. Conversely, if his horse is a good weight-carrier, he may gain an advantage in finding a race where all the horses must carry heavy weights. There probably will be some horses in that race which will be at a disadvantage, thus giving his horse a more favorable opportunity to win.

It is important that you find a jockey who can make the weight assigned your horse. That one extra pound may cost you the race. Occasionally you may be forced to carry a little extra weight, but it would be wiser of you to take advantage of all the allowances to which your horse is entitled. There is little question that carrying extra weight is a disadvantage, particularly if you expect to race the horse in handicap races at a future date. It raises his handicap weight by just that much and you cannot afford to give away weight unnecessarily. The question of "live" versus "dead" weight is strictly a matter of opinion. The author is undecided in this matter.

When all the above has been taken into consideration, along with the conditions of the race, the trainer will make a "guesstimate" as to the correctness of his placement of the horse in that race. The above conditions plus the inevitable "racing luck" are items that will enable one set of "four fleet feet" to reach the winner's circle.

8
The Use of Drugs in Training

Too many times thoroughbreds are subjected to training or racing when they are not fit. If a horse is not in a reasonable state of fitness, he should not be in training. The author fully realizes that the "time and money" theory is involved because the general upkeep of a racing thoroughbred is expensive, especially when he is not racing. Therefore, "time" causes trainers to rush getting their horses to the races. Unfortunately, this thinking many times causes a horse to break down completely and the trainer will get no use at all out of his thoroughbred for an extended period of time.

If a horse must be rushed into training, there are various therapeutic drugs that will aid in a more speedy recovery. Butazolidin, for example, not only alleviates pain, but also has a therapeutic affect on cases of degenerative arthritis. While a horse is being trained on "beauts," he feels little or no pain and also gets the benefit of the drug's aid in the recuperating process. A relatively high dose is administered during the first 48 hours and then reduced gradually to a maintenance level. The lowest dose possible is used to hold the symptoms in check. In the treatment of inflammatory conditions with an infection basis, supportive antibacterial therapy is recommended. The combined action of butazolidin and corticosteroids has been successfully used in humans. In horses, butazolidin is largely metabolized in eight hours. Best results are obtained by giving ½ the daily dose at 12-hour intervals. The immediate response to butazolidin therapy is prompt and usually occurs within 24 hours. However, if no response is evident after five days, it is suggested that the treatment be discontinued. Butazolidin may be administered either orally or intravenously. In some instances, the tablets may be crushed and given with feed. The dosage should be reduced as the symptoms decrease. In long-term therapy, oral administration of butazolidin is suggested.

However, too much of a drug of this sort will result in a thinning of the blood. If too much work is given the thoroughbred at this time, he could eventually break down and therefore negate the earlier values of the treatment that was administered. Any drug that removes or alleviates pain in the training period has to be of value, especially if recuperative values are also associated with the drug. "Beauts" are illegal in most states when used during racing and should only be used when rehabilitating a horse. It is important to remember that if a horse is sore, the cause should be ascertained and then proper treatment should be administered. Butazolidin is an effective medication for the various muscle and joint aches of your thoroughbred. It greatly relieves the swelling, fever and arthritic conditions of most horses. A result is the lessening of the condition which causes pain; thus your horse will be able to perform up to his ability.

Phenylbutazone is another drug which is easily detected

and can be qualitatively evaluated in tests. In the same manner, the steroids are hormonal, anti-inflammatory, anti-pyretic, anti-arthritic medications, and are sometimes of aid in rehabilitating horses. Steroids, unfortunately, have side affects which can destroy bone tissue and can weaken the horse's natural ability to produce its own steroids. It is the opinion of the author that butazolidin is less harmful than phenylbutazone and steroids.

In the case of new, minor injuries, any of the anti-inflammatory drugs are of value as they reduce swelling and keep pain to a minimum. It is important to remember that when using any of the forbidden drugs in the treatment of injuries, they can be traced up to 72 hours after the last administration. Sometimes, there is a residual showing even after that period. When in doubt, a vet should be consulted as to the usage and probable effects relating to the drug. It is much wiser to seek the advice of a vet in what drug to use and also seek him to administer the drug. If you should administer the drug and the horse should die, the insurance would not pay the owner. If a vet administers a drug and the horse should die, the insurance company will pay for the loss.

A combination of vitamins usually comprise what is commonly called a "cocktail." Many legal "cocktails" are administered by vets at race tracks and these may greatly aid in a thoroughbred's performance. "Cocktails" are sometimes given a horse after an exceedingly hard race in order to "pick him up." These are legal and will not result in the racing commission suspending the person caring for the horse or revoking the purse monies won.

Unfortunately, new drugs are being developed far faster than the ability to detect them. This, unfortunately, brings about illegal usage by some unscrupulous persons in an effort to beat detection. Again, the vet should be requested to give the horse whatever legal medical help he can before the race. The investment is a wise one.

Consult the vet for clinical observations concerning new drugs and keep informed by reading as much as you can of the related literature in this field.

Vets are trained specialists; they are the most knowledgeable persons available in this field and they should constantly be contacted in relation to the use of any drug.

There are two important points being stressed in this chapter. First, whenever possible, horses should be raced only when fit and, secondly, that a vet should be consulted for the administration of any drug.

9
Horse Ailments and Treatments

This chapter deals with the more common ailments found in horses and the treatment of these conditions.

Fever, excessive fluid, and calcification may occur in various places in the horse, as may muscle, tendon, ligament, and bone problems. The condition, or ailment, may in reality be the same. But, the location is different, hence the difference in terminology. However, in the terminology used regarding the treatment, the terms remain constant and mean the same at all times. At this point a description of the terms most frequently used will be given.

BLISTER

A horse may be blistered for one of many reasons. The primary reason is that a blister acts as a counter-irritant to pain and assists in the removal of a synovial deposit. This deposit presents an amount of excessive fluid or calcification. The effect of the blister is to draw blood to the affected area, thus hastening the process of repair.

Blisters may also be used after surgery has been performed. The surgery may have caused much separation and movement of muscles, tendons or ligaments. After the normal recuperative process has taken place, a horse may be blistered with the hope that all the physical parts in the affected area will, after the blister, return to their normal positions.

A Harvey's Blister is an example of a commercial blister often used. In the case of blistering the knee, the blister takes hold in a couple of hours. The knee then starts to swell and by the next morning it will be twice its normal size. In a few days the pockets of inflammation will start to break open and ooze yellow pus. This is indicative of the blister's effective work. When the injury is distended, or blown up, it can be likened to a balloon full of air. When the air is released, the balloon returns to its normal size and shape. The same is hoped of the blister. It is hoped that all parts in the injured area will return to their normal position.

The secondary purpose of the blister presupposes that two fevers cannot occupy the same place at the same time. Through the usage of the blister, a second artificial fever is introduced. This higher fever drives out the infection or fever already present. The artificial fever, by nature of its being artificial, will leave itself. It is hoped that all deep fever is gone, all former parts are back in place, and that the injured area has returned to its normal size. After a gap of a couple of months, when the injury or inflammation had been great, the affected area may sometimes be re-blistered. In some instances, as in the case of knee blistering, the opposite knee may also be blistered to prevent the horse from shifting all weight to the good knee and, in time, injuring the good knee. Because there would have been extreme pain in the blistered knee, the horse would have been inclined to place all its weight on the other knee, thus probably damaging the good knee before the original blister was over. The act of blistering the good knee, in this example, would also freshen and take out any fever that might have been present in the good knee. The Harvey's Blister is an example of a quick, severe blister that leaves no scars.

A Red Mercury Blister is another type of blister. The Red Mercury salve is rubbed in and covered with bandages for about ten days. When the bandages are removed the result should be the same as in other types of blisters.

When blistering such areas as the knee, particular attention should be made not to blister the point of the knee, the bump or back part of the knee that sticks out. Vaseline, or the like, should be applied to avoid blistering of that area, or a delay in healing of up to six months could take place. Vasoline should be applied to other specific areas not to be blistered.

There is no specific blistering agent which can be specified as the best one for usage. Choice is dependent on the nature of the injury and the person treating it. Experience, unfortunately many times by trial and error, will enable those treating the injury to determine what works most effectively for them.

Some generalizations concerning blistering would be: do not blister until the affected part has thoroughly cooled and feels cold to the touch, shave the area to be blistered, and protect, by vaseline or the like, areas you do not want blistered. Finally, choose the type of blister you feel is needed, such as a long or short blister, deep or surface, etc.

POULTICE

While a blister tends to introduce an artificial fever to

the affected area, a poultice is used to draw out minor inflammation. A poultice is a kind of balm or salve which is applied to the affected area in the form of a dressing. It may be composed of many types of ingredients varying from clay or mud 'to antiseptic-type poultices. Again, the type of poultice used should be indicated by the nature of the soreness and inflammation.

ANTISEPTICS

Various commercial antiseptics are used for minor cuts and abrasions as indicated. The nature and severity of the injury determines the antiseptic used.

FIRING

Firing is the term used when an "iron" is applied. Firing causes more than deep blistering or cauterizing. Firing is usually performed when there has been severe damage to musculature. The desired result of the firing is to fasten one muscle to another with the aid of scar tissue. Theoretically, firing goes much beyond blistering because it fastens tissue to tissue. In this process, the weak and strong tissues are fastened together with the aid of scar tissue. All of these tissues then aid in supporting each other. Time is necessary in the strengthening process after firing.

PAINT

The term "painting" is used when a combination of various ingredients are applied directly to the affected area and serve as a minor counter-irritant.

The next portion of this chapter deals, in alphabetical

order, with many of the more common horse ailments or conditions which hamper or stop a horse from performing adequately.

BLEEDER

A bleeder is a horse that bleeds in the nasal area during or after a workout or race. This condition is the result of a rupture of a blood vessel, usually the trifacial veins, in the nose. This condition, if not hereditary, can be the result of demanding too much from a horse or racing a horse that is unfit. The excessive strain placed by either case causes the rupture and resultant bleeding which immediately impairs the horse's breathing and makes it impossible for him to continue running at peak performance.

It is possible to cure horses that have had a bleeding problem. Coagulants are often the immediate, but only temporary, treatment. Asking the horse for what he is capable is one reasonable assurance of not having a constantly recurring bleeding problem. An increasingly more difficult and demanding training program, rather than "crash training," may eventually lead to maximum performance and efficiency within the limitations of the horse.

BOG SPAVIN

A bog spavin is a chronic, puffy swelling located on the inside and a little in front of the hock. Although the horse may have good hocks, a bog spavin may occur as a result of undue concussion or strain and eventually lead to lameness. When in this stage, no calcification has taken place. The condition results because of leakage from the synovial joint.

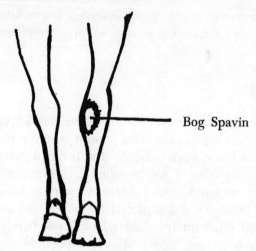

Bog Spavin

Diagram 1:
Bog Spavin

Treatment: If the swelling is small, work can continue. If large, the horse should be rested. When small, paint the horse with a solution of iodine, Reducine, or similar paints. If large, blister every six weeks until swelling becomes smaller or disappears.

BONE SPAVIN

A bone spavin is a bony growth inside and just below the hock. Unlike the bog spavin, which is soft, calcification has taken place and a bony growth has developed. This condition need not be of a serious nature until it causes lameness.

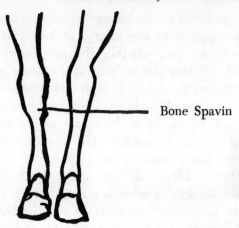

Bone Spavin

Diagram 2:
Bone Spavin

Treatment: Cool the injury out. Rest and turn out for six months. Use ice packs, whirlpool, epsom salts, ammonium chloride, refrigerants, etc. to cool out the injury. When finally cooled out, the horse may be blistered or fired. The heels of the shoe may also be raised.

BOWED TENDON

This term indicates a rupture of the sheath which encloses the flexor tendon, running from the knee to the fetlock joint. A bowed tendon may be caused by strain placed on the tendons as the horse leaves his position at a dead gallop or, occasionally, when a horse strains to get out of the heavy going or mud. The tendon, when loosened from the cannon bone, gives the appearance of a bow string drawn back from the wood of the bow itself.

Bowed tendons vary according to the degree of their severity. They may be slight, or hopeless from the beginning. The secondary conditions accompanying the bow indicate the severity of the injury. Included in these secondary conditions are: whether the suspensory ligaments are involved, whether one or both of the flexor tendons are involved, whether the injury is high and involves the check ligaments at the top of the knee, whether the injury involves the suspensory ligaments at the sesamoids, or whether the injury is below the sesamoids. The reader must keep in mind that the flexor tendons run all the way to the toe of the foot. Thus, a horse can bow above the fetlock, in the middle of the tendon, or what is termed a high bow, which goes up into the check ligaments. When the bow involves the check ligaments, the prognosis is unfavorable. A middle or low bow has a better prognosis.

In the matter of all bowed tendons, a long period of rest is indicated. By rest, it is implied that the horse should be turned out, not allowed to stand in a stall. The horse should be allowed to move. It is believed, by the author, that the tendon will heal better and become stronger when the horse is allowed to move. While immobilization will result in faster healing, strength (due to inactivity), will be lacking. Horses should be turned out for three to four months before blistering.

Cross-firing is the type of firing performed on bowed horses. The theory is that the cross-firing acts the same as putting on a permanent bandage. Scar lines are applied with the iron at angles. As they heal, they pull together and pull in and up to form scar tissue which should pull the whole leg back into its former position. Given enough time, the scar tissue will form a permanent bandage on the leg. The scar tissue is much stronger than the ordinary tissue but does not have the elasticity. The scar lines serve to tighten the whole leg.

In order to effectively treat bowed horses, the cause of the bow should be ascertained. If the cause still exists, remove that cause. Treatment of the injury will prove futile if the cause is not removed, and the horse will probably rebow.

If there is the slightest indication that a horse has rapped itself, he should be stopped and sweated with a light blister and slowly put back to work in ten days, a good horse in thirty days.

It is also the opinion of the author that the amount of work that is done with the hands, the amount of personal rubbing, is as important as what is applied.

A bowed horse is never the same horse he was before. When returned to racing, he usually has a chance in races that are run for less than one-half of the claiming price he ran for before. Bowed horses can run and win again, but very rarely at the same "class" as before.

A bowed horse, when he extends himself, may rebow. These types of horses should never be raced in the mud or on tracks with holes.

A generalization that may be made is that horses that have had knee or bowed tendon injuries should be raced on a hard, fast track. On this type of track the horse does not have to flex the knee too much. He runs in a gliding motion. A fairly level, firm turf course would also be fine to run these types of horses.

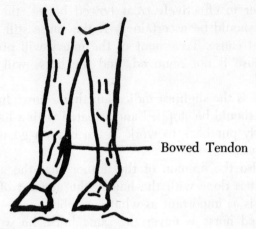

Bowed Tendon

Diagram 3:
Bowed Tendon

Treatment: In most cases, blistering or firing must be done and the horse turned out for a long period of rest.

Bowed tendon.

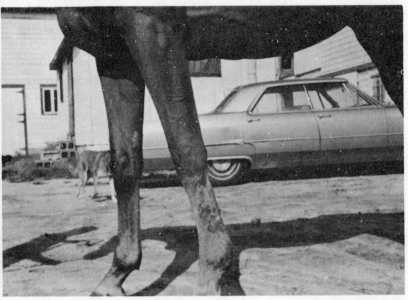

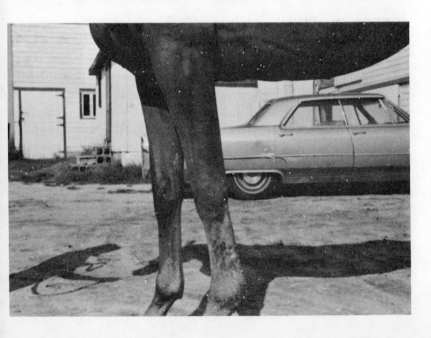

BRITTLE FEET

This term is used when there is a dry condition of the horn of the foot.

A horse, in his natural state, can be found walking around in the dew every morning. It is natural for the horse's feet to be wet and damp. Nature produces an oil to keep the feet lubricated. But, when placed in a stall, no moisture gets into the feet. Grease or petroleum products are used to overcome this lack of moisture. When too much of this foot ointment is used, nature stops producing the natural oil and dry feet ensue. Sea water and sand are also believed to cause this condition. If the horse's feet are properly washed and dried every morning in fresh water, and ointment is applied only once a week, dry feet should not occur. A little fungicide, or something in the nature of Clorox, added to the water would make a good washing solution.

BROKEN WIND

Broken wind is a breakdown of the air vesicles of the lungs caused by too much strain being placed upon them. This is usually caused by strain or excessive feeding before exercise. There is usually nothing that will cure a broken-winded horse, but the condition may be lessened by special feedings. It is possible to get some racing out of a broken-winded horse, assuming the condition is not too severe.

BRUSHING

Brushing is an injury to the fetlock caused by a strike

from the opposite foot. It should be treated as a bruise or wound. This usually occurs in horses that are in poor or weak condition, but may also be caused by poor shoeing. If the cause of this condition can be prevented, no such injury will occur. Brushing only occurs in the process of running. A leather boot should be put over the area where the horse's other foot strikes.

CANKER

Canker is a softening of the horn of the foot forming a moist, cheese-like growth with a particularly objectionable smell. Canker is usually found where horses are kept under poor conditions, such as poorly-drained stables.

The condition generally starts in the frog, extends to the sole, and the horn becomes soddened with a moist growth which, in time, can be squeezed out at the sole. Canker can be likened to an abscess or sore found deep in the feet. In treating, part of the foot may have to be removed. In washing the feet, water with fungicide added may help act as a preventative. Unless caused by a concussion, horses should never get canker where wholesome stable habits are performed. Canker can usually be cured by an antibiotic.

CAPPED HOCK

This condition is caused by a horse kicking or rubbing his hocks while in the stall. This is a bruise. An analgesic balm, liniment, or other type of paint will aid in the treatment. This condition is basically an eyesore. Capped hocks have little effect on performance. If the condition becomes calloused, blistering may be performed.

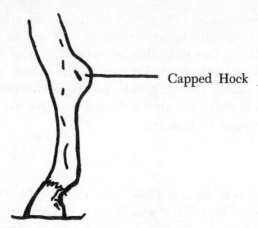

Capped Hock

Diagram 4:
Capped Hock

Treatment: If recent, use a liniment, balm, or other type of paint. Any of the commercial products may do. If calloused, blistering may be indicated.

CORN

The causes of corns in horses are the same as in humans. Undue pressure by the shoe on the seat of the injury, due to poor shoeing or shoes that have been left on too long, cause corns. This condition is actually a bruise of the sensitive sole in the angle formed by the bar and the wall. In horses that are unshod, little or no corns are found. Corns may be detected by their reddish color, which is due to the presence of blood in the area.

Seat of the corn

Diagram 5:
Seat of the corn

Treatment: Remove the shoe and reduce inflammation. This may be best accomplished by means of hot antiseptic poultices which should be renewed once or twice a day until the inflammation and soreness is gone. Then have the corn cut out.

COW HOCKS

This condition exists when the points of the hocks are turned in. Cow hocks are part of a horse's conformation.

CRIB-BITER

A crib-biter swallows air by catching hold of the manger or another convenient object with his teeth. This is discouraged by using creosote or covering objects with metal. Crib-biting is a habit acquired by a horse that is bored and has nothing to do. This condition can give rise to indigestion and eventually cause an unsoundness.

In a former court case, this condition was legally stated to be an unsoundness and should a horse be a "cribber," a statement of this must be made in the sale of that horse.

CURB

The cause of curb is difficult to ascertain. It can usually be attributed to undue strain. Basically, it is a sprain at the back of the hock. It is common in young jumping horses.

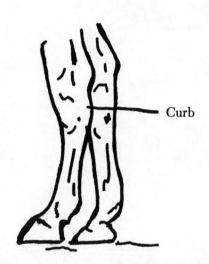

Curb

Diagram 6:
Curb

Treatment: Rest the heel with calkins or a wedge-shaped shoe. Apply ice or cold water. If necessary, apply a blister or such preparations as iodine ointment, Radiol, or Reducine, which should be rubbed in thoroughly for several days (not after the skin has cracked). Firing will seldom fail to effect a permanent cure.

FALSE QUARTER

A false quarter is a horizontal crack in the hoof and is

caused by an injury to the coronet. The secretion of the horn is checked. To treat, a new horn formation is encouraged by the application of a red blister to the coronet. This condition is much rarer than the vertical quarter crack.

GRUNTING

It is generally thought that a horse that "grunts" may or may not be unsound in the wind. A horse may be thick-in-the-wind when gross and fat. When this condition exists, the horse should not be given work requiring speed.

KNEE SPAVIN

A knee spavin is a bony growth at the back of the knee and on the inner side. It is caused by a blow or by a strain. Treat by blistering or firing. This is another of the spavin injuries and must be treated accordingly. The term knee indicates the location of the injury.

LAMINITIS

Laminitis is an inflammation of the sensitive parts directly under the horny wall of the foot. It is a serious and painful disease, and is more common in front than behind. A horse that has laminitis is commonly termed "foundered." This is a chronic, acute inflammation of the laminae, or soft tissue of the foot and is incurable. A horse may have laminitis in varying degrees. Actually, the sole drops and the horse is standing on the coffin bone which causes extreme pain. Either block heels or leather pads should be put on to get the horse up off the ground.

Laminitis is progressive. Some causes of the disease are:

any high fever such as caused by pneumonia or another disease, a horse that was improperly cooled out, a horse that was given too much cold water after a workout, a horse that was fed while still warm, or forage (food) poisoning. The point being made is that, as in people, a fever may lead to other diseases, such as laminitis in a horse.

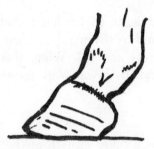

Diagram 7:
The concave and ringed appearance of the foot following acute laminitis

NAVICULAR DISEASE

Navicular Disease is one of the most common and most serious diseases that a horse may get. Actually, since there is no known cure, the disease eventually results in death. Briefly, it is a corrosive ulcer on the navicular bone, and is practically confined to the fore feet. (This bone is found centrally in the foot (L in the diagram below).

The ball joint of the navicular bone does not get enough fluid to function properly. Movement causes friction, pain, swelling, and loss of action. When the horse is laid off, he apparently becomes sound again. This is because the joint binds only when the horse is in action. But, when the horse is returned to action and runs again, he will again suffer due to the friction in the joint. This disease is a hopeless, progressive condition. Neurotomy, commonly called nerving, is the surgical cutting or severing of a nerve to relieve pain. Heel nerving may allay this condition, but the end result will be the same. However, heel nerving only takes care of the back half of the foot. If the trouble is in the front half, one must nerve the plantar nerve above the ankle.

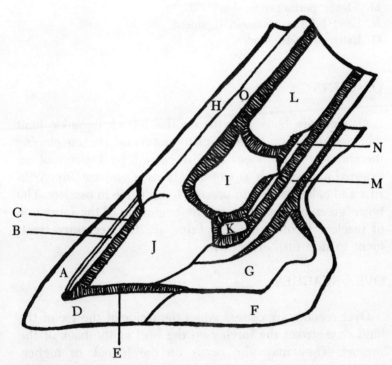

Diagram 8:
Vertical section locating the pedal bones
A. Crust or wall
B. Insensitive lamine

C. Sensitive lamine
D. Insensitive sole
E. Sensitive sole
F. Insensitive frog
G. Sensitive frog
H. Coronary band
I. Short pastern bone
J. Coffin bone
K. Navicular bone
L. Long pastern bone
M. Flexor perforans tendon
N. Long inferior sesamoid ligament
O. Extensor pedis tendon

OSSELETS

Osselets are bony growths on the fetlock or ankle joint which usually result from inflammation of the enveloping membrane of the bone. This is caused by injuries of an external nature, such as wounds, bruises, and sprains. Arthritis and calcification are present to a degree in osselets. The term "green osselets" implies the beginning of the formation of osselets. Cooling out and firing are the necessary treatment to stop further growth.

OVER-REACHES

Over-reaches are caused when the inside of the toe of the hind shoe strikes the foreleg on the heel or the back of the coronet. They may also occur on the fetlock or higher. Usually over-reaches occur while a horse is jumping or when the going is deep. When they occur, iodine should be applied immediately and the injury treated as a wound. Over-reaches may also be due to faulty shoeing or poor conformation. If the cause is removed, the condition should be non-existent. A boot may be used to alleviate the problem.

QUARTER-CRACK OR "SAND CRACK"

A quarter-crack is a vertical crack in the wall of the hoof running downward from the coronet to the ground or, in some cases, only a part of the way down. The horse may or may not go lame.

Treatment: Remove all pressure from the crack. A clamp may be put across the crack. The coronet may be blistered to stimulate the growth of a new horn. Certain oil-based products can alleviate this condition. A patch may be applied.

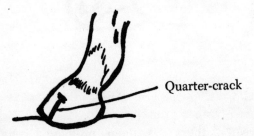

Quarter-crack

Diagram 9:
Quarter-crack

RING-BONE

A bony enlargement around the top of the hoof or near the pastern bones is termed "ringbone." This condition is common in horses where the pasterns are too straight, thus causing excessive jarring on the bone. It may also be caused by a blow or when the shoes are not removed at regular intervals, thus allowing the heels to grow too long. This is another example of friction causing excessive fluid which eventually leads to calcification.

Treatment: Rest the horse with its shoes removed and put him on a laxative diet. Use a whirlpool twice a day. Blistering, under the advice of a vet, may help. Nerving is a drastic remedy which is sometimes performed, but not recommended. Firing around the coffin bone may aid in the treatment.

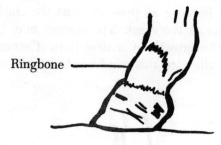

Ringbone

Diagram 10:
Ringbone

REARING

In a "rearer" there is a deep, prolonged cough usually heard when a horse is galloping or racing. It can be either very audible or hardly audible, depending upon the gravity of the condition. A horse that is kept fit will make less noise than one that is unfit. The only possible treatment for cure is an operation. The earlier performed, the more likely the chance of its being successful. Even if the operation is not fully successful, the overall condition of the horse should be improved. However, in the case of "cheap" horses, the gamble may not be practical.

SESAMOIDITIS

Sesamoiditis is an inflammation of the bones situated just above and below the fetlock joint. "Cracked sesamoids," or sesamoiditis, presents a problem of varying degree. Some of the problems involved are: where the fracture is located, whether it is compound, whether there is a separation, is it a chip, or is it a hairline fracture on the apex where healing would take place naturally? The answers to these questions can only be ascertained through X rays. The sesamoids are not fastened to anything. They are the pulley for the suspensory ligaments. The suspensory ligaments come down from behind the knee, then around the sesamoids, and fasten to the coronet band.

Whether to train or race a horse with this condition is strictly a wild guess, regardless of whether the decision is made by a vet or the trainer. Some horses will remain in racing with a large sesamoid separation, while others with hardly visible hairline fractures cannot stand.

Treatment: Rest and blister or pin-fire. But there is no certain cure.

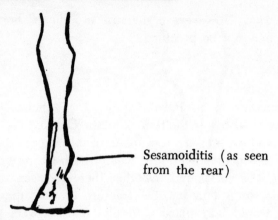

Sesamoiditis (as seen from the rear)

Diagram 11:
Sesamoiditis (as seen from the rear)

SHOE BOIL

A shoe boil is termed a "capped elbow." This is a serious enlargement on the point of the elbow which is caused by bruising from the shoe while lying down or being allowed to lay down in a stall with insufficient bedding. The heel of the shoe may be knocked off, or a cap or "donut" applied to help alleviate this condition.

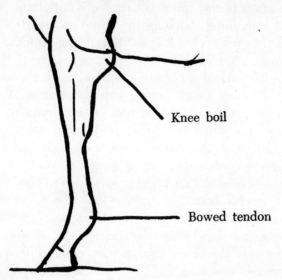

Diagram 12:
Knee boil
Bowed tendon

SPEEDY CUT

A speedy cut is an injury to the knee or hock caused by a strike from the opposite foot. Treatment would be the same as if treating for a bruise or wound.

SPLINTS

A splint is a bony growth on the side of the splint bone. This condition is more common on the inside than the outside of the leg. Splints appear more often in younger horses and are generally caused by the horse's legs being jarred while still young. This is another case of calcification.

The location of the splint is extremely important. Whether there is something touching the splint or whether it is far enough forward so that it is not interfering with the suspensory ligament or extensor tendon is indicative of the treatment to be used. If the splint does not touch the aforementioned, it is not much more than an eyesore. Once the growth has stopped, there should be no problem.

Pain occurs when the splint pushes against the periosteum. As long as the growth continues, pain will continue. X rays are not needed to see splints.

A horse can run a race and a splint may cause the horse not to give his best. But by the time the horse is pulled up, turned around, and unsaddled, he may appear sound due to the pressure being taken off. The horse may or may not be sore to the touch. Splints may cause other problems in horses by nature of the horse putting its weight on its other leg due to pain from a splint.

Splints may be a major problem if not treated to stop further calcification. Firing in the center of the splint is recommended for this purpose. If the splint is small, a whirlpool might help. In more persistent cases, blistering or firing, as indicated above, must be performed. The horse should be given as much work as he can take.

STRING HALT

String halt is a nervous condition causing involuntary elevation of the hind legs. There is no treatment known to cure a horse with this condition. Operations are only recommended in the case of very valuable show horses. This condition detracts little, if at all, from the usefulness of the horse.

THOROUGHPINS

This condition is similar to a bog spavin. It occurs on the upper and back part of the hock. Swelling often goes all the way through . . . hence the name thoroughpins. This condition seldom causes lameness. If small, no treatment is necessary. If large, blister and repeat every six weeks until the swelling lessens and disappears.

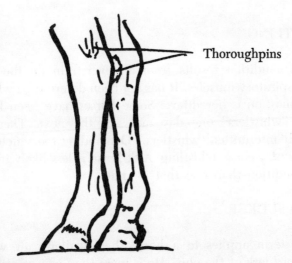

Thoroughpins

Diagram 13:
Thoroughpins

THRUSH

Thrush is a fungus infection or inflammation of the frog, with symptoms rather like those of Canker. Thrush is primarily found in the cleft of the frog. It can be likened to athlete's foot in humans. This condition is found in horses that have been standing in badly drained stables or stalls that have not been mucked out for periods of time. Thrush may, or may not, cause lameness. This depends on the severity of the infection. A very foul smell accompanies this condition. The feet should be washed thoroughly with either a disinfectant or fungicide added to the water. In bad cases, pare out the frog and apply antiseptics into the cavity. Repeat. Thrush, if discovered in time, is relatively easy to cure.

WHISTLING

This condition results from an overstrain on the lungs and respiratory muscles. It has not been determined whether this condition is hereditary. Some horses have been known to be "whistlers" one day and not the next. These are termed "intermittent whistlers." Demanding too much from a horse may cause whistling. A fit horse is less likely to have this condition than one that is unfit.

WIND SUCKER

This term applies to a horse that swallows air with a backward jerk of the chin. He is more than just a "cribber." This condition is discouraged by placing a strap around the thin part of the neck, tight enough to prevent contraction of the muscles.

REVIEW OF LOCATIONS OF LEG INJURIES

The diagram below reviews some of the locations of the various injuries described in this chapter.

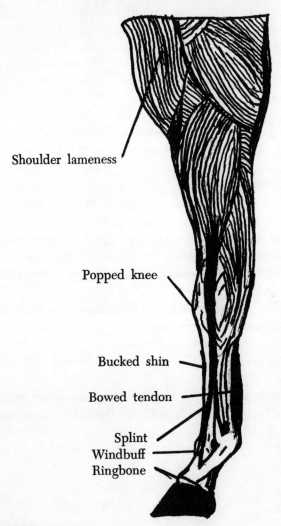

Shoulder lameness

Popped knee

Bucked shin

Bowed tendon

Splint
Windbuff
Ringbone

Diagram 14:
Shoulder lameness
Popped knee
Bucked shin

Bowed tendon
Splint
Windbuff
Ringbone

SUMMARY

The various treatments suggested in this chapter are not intended to negate the importance of the veterinarian. Certainly, whenever there is any doubt, a vet should be consulted immediately.

Constant attention must be given to the horses in your care. If this is properly done, many of the causes of injuries will be removed. However careful, injuries are still bound to occur. This chapter suggested some of the more universally accepted terms and treatments now being used in the industry.

As stated at the beginning of this chapter, knowledge and experience are extremely important in the correct diagnosis of the nature and extent of the injury or ailment. Effort and hard work are necessary tools for effectively administering treatment.

Your dedication to the pursuance of the above will result in both a better horse and a better man.

10
Racing Luck

It is hoped that upon reaching this chapter all concerned will understand that there is no exclusive clause guaranteeing a horse will win.

Be it a minor or major injury, be it poor training, be it an injury of any nature or just bad luck, the day will come when the gates will open and the announcer will say "they're off." At that point, with your heart in your mouth, you will be the complete and unwilling victim of the age-old dictum called "racing luck." You may have the best horse in the race and lose, yet on another day you will win because of "racing luck." Yes, there are many more factors involved. One stone on the track, no racing room, a poor ride, too much weight, or any one of so many other factors may negate all the work and effort put into the thoroughbred in order that he might possess "four fleet feet."

[Good luck!]

Index

83